C000102244

The

The Sayings of

DISRAELI

edited by

ROBERT BLAKE

DUCKWORTH

First published in 1992 by
Gerald Duckworth & Co. Ltd.
The Old Piano Factory
48 Hoxton Square, London N1 6PB

Introduction and editorial arrangement
© 1992 by Robert Blake

A catalogue record for this book is available
from the British Library

ISBN 0 7156 2424 7

Photoset in North Wales by
Derek Doyle & Associates, Mold, Clwyd
Printed in Great Britain by
Redwood Press Limited, Melksham

Contents

Dedicated to
George Burnett and Arthur Dodds
companions in our escape from Italy
1943–44

Introduction

Benjamin Disraeli (1804-1881), first and last Earl of
Beaconsfield, was the only Victorian Prime Minister to be
educated neither at a public school nor a university. His
father Isaac, a literary man of private means, was of
Sephardic Jewish upbringing, but a Deist by inclination. He
quarrelled with the local synagogue at Bevis Marks in East
London, and had his children – Benjamin was the eldest
son – baptized and confirmed as Anglicans. This chance of
events was crucial in Benjamin's political career. He
entered Parliament in 1837. The barrier against non-
Christians was only lifted twenty-one years later. But
Disraeli, as some of these 'sayings' show, was a very
unorthodox Anglican and remained always fascinated by
the connection between Judaism and Christianity. 'I am the
blank page between the Old and New Testament' – so he is
supposed to have said to Queen Victoria.

Disraeli would be an important figure in history even if,
like most Prime Ministers, he had never written a word for
publication. Neither Walpole, the two Pitts, Peel, nor
Palmerston wrote much except for official purposes.
Gladstone did, but most of it is unreadable. 'The Sayings of
Mr Gladstone' would not get many buyers. The 3rd
Marquis of Salisbury was an able and acid political
commentator when, as an impoverished younger son, he
needed to earn money. Lord Rosebery wrote a few brilliant
vignettes, notably an unforgettable short essay on Lord
Randolph Churchill. Alas, his masterpiece according to his
biographer, Sir Robert Rhodes James, has not seen the light
of day. Perhaps not surprisingly in view of its title:
'Copulation Ancient and Modern' – a spoof lecture
allegedly delivered jointly by Ferdinand de Rothschild and
the future Edward VII at the Imperial Institute. Many later

Prime Ministers have written their memoirs – mostly dull, long-winded and self-exculpatory – with one exception, Winston Churchill, who was a writer of genius and did not confine himself to memoirs.

Churchill and Disraeli stand out in the long line of occupants of 10 Downing Street as the only two who could be described as professional authors. They wrote for the same reason, exemplifying Dr Johnson's dictum 'No man but a blockhead ever wrote except for money'. Churchill was far more successful than Disraeli. He probably made more in real terms than any other non-fiction writer in the twentieth century. It was only late in life that Disraeli struck modest oil. *Lothair* (1870), the collected novels published in the same year, together with *Endymion* (1880) brought him in at least £20,000 – the equivalent of over three quarters of a million today. The novels which he wrote with almost frenetic energy between 1826 and 1837 did little more than stave off temporarily the more urgent of his creditors. He had incurred a load of debt as a result of reckless speculation on the Stock Exchange. Aggravated by his personal extravagance and only in part relieved by his marriage to a rich widow in 1839, the load was to encumber him long past middle age. The famous trilogy, *Coningsby* (1844), *Sybil* (1845) and *Tancred* (1847), was not notably rewarding in money terms, about £1,000 for each of the first two and £750 for the last.

By this stage Disraeli had become a well-known, though not a well-trusted, figure. His dubious three-cornered relationship in the 1830s with his mistress, Lady Sykes, and his patron, the ex-Lord Chancellor, Lord Lyndhurst, was not forgotten, nor were his extravagance, his debts, the fiasco of his maiden speech, and his denial in 1846 of having asked Peel for office in 1841 – a lie and widely known to be one. The Protectionist Conservatives enjoyed the matter of his bitter diatribes against Peel over the Corn Laws but not the manner. However, when the great divide occurred they had only two men of ability on their side. Lord Derby, who led them, was in the Lords. There was no option but to put up with Disraeli in the Commons.

There was a long haul ahead. As time passed the aura of mistrust which hung about him gradually faded, but acceptance by his party did not bring political success for many years. The Conservatives were the minority party from 1846 to 1886 and only once had a working majority in all that time, when Disraeli won the election of 1874. There were three short-lived Conservative governments, 1852, 1858-9 and 1866-8. In each of them Disraeli was Chancellor of the Exchequer and in the last ten months of the third he reached 'the top of the greasy pole' as Prime Minister.

In these years he wrote nothing except his *Life of Lord George Bentinck* – a source for many of his 'sayings'. But after 1868 Gladstone's clear victory gave him leisure to produce *Lothair*, and another defeat allowed him to write *Endymion* just before he died. His last authorial fling was *Falconet*, a thinly veiled lampoon on Gladstone. It is unfinished and was posthumously first published in *The Times* on 20, 21 and 23 January 1905. Its nine short chapters show no sign of flagging powers and are in some places very amusing.

Disraeli remains, despite all that he wrote and has been written about him, something of an enigma. That he had extraordinary talents cannot be doubted. The Victorian era was not as rigid, hide-bound or conventional as it is sometimes depicted. But, with every allowance made, one must be astonished at the rise of the extravagant, flamboyant, novel-writing son of a Jewish littérateur to become leader of the Party of Old England, Prime Minister and favourite statesman of Queen Victoria. It was a romantic and dramatic story. No one was more conscious of this than Disraeli himself. He was aware that he was unique. He was intensely egotistical – of course most politicians are or they would not be politicians – and he was constantly surveying himself in mirrors – tinted sometimes with romance, sometimes irony, sometimes cynicism. Life to him was a many-coloured drama in which he was the actor-manager. Even if he could not always manage he could always act. What he really thought about anything is far from clear. He probably did not know himself.

More than most politicians of the past and unlike nearly all those of today, he believed in the importance of language. 'With words we govern men.' Churchill has been the only statesman of the twentieth century to act on that principle. Their words are remembered. Who remembers those of Clement Attlee or Anthony Eden? Not that a politician's achievement should be judged by that criterion. There are many others. The wits and aphorists are not qualified to govern their country simply because of those gifts, but it adds to the gaiety of nations when they do. And Disraeli and Churchill did it rather well.

Disraeli's particular brand of 'sayings' is not quite like those of anyone else, whether politician, poet or dramatist. There is perhaps an element of Thomas Love Peacock in some of his novels. Byron certainly influenced him. They never met, though the poet was at least an acquaintance and something of an admirer of Isaac D'Israeli, who was a best-selling anthologist of literary observations and anecdotes. Disraeli's wit was more like that of Oscar Wilde than anyone else, but of course the debt was Wilde's not Disraeli's. What still fascinates one about Disraeli's observations, which are by no means all witticisms, is their timeless quality of penetration, humour, irreverence and paradox. Of course it provoked fury among the *bien pensant* Victorians. Trollope led the field: 'The wit has been the wit of hairdressers and the enterprise the enterprise of mountebanks.' I do not know many mountebanks, but if the numerous men who have cut my hair over the years had had one tenth of the wit of Disraeli, I would have no complaints.

References and Abbreviations

B = Blake, *Disraeli* (1966); CP = Blake, *Conservative Party from Peel to Thatcher* (1985); DD = Fraser, *Disraeli and his Day* (1891); DG = Blake, *Disraeli and Gladstone* (1969); DGT = Blake *Disraeli's Grand Tour* (1982); LGB = Disraeli, *Life of Lord George Bentinck* (4th ed. revised 1852); M & B = Monypenny and Buckle, *Life of Disraeli* 6 vols. (1910-1920); MD = Wilfrid Meynell, *The Man Disraeli* (revised ed. 1927); R = Disraeli's Reminiscences ed. H. and M. Schwartz (1971); WW = *Wit and Wisdom of Lord Beaconsfield*, anon. but, in fact, edited by Sir H. Calcraft (1881); Z = *Letters of Disraeli to Lady Bradford and Lady Chesterfield*, ed. Lord Zetland (1929).

Disraeli's speeches are identified by place and date of delivery – H of C, or H of L and speeches outside Parliament by city or town. References to novels are given by title, 'book', or 'part', and 'chapter', but not by page number because of the numerous editions. The novels with dates of first publication are: *Vivian Grey* (1826-7); *Popanilla* (1828); *The Young Duke* (1831); *Contarini Fleming* (1832); *Alroy* and *The Rise of Iskander* in one volume (1833); *Henrietta Temple* (1837); *Venetia* (1837); *Coningsby* (1844); *Sybil* (1845); *Tancred* (1847); *Lothair* (1870); *Endymion* (1880); *Falconet* unfinished and first published in *The Times* (1905), later in the Bradenham Edition of the Novels ed. Philip Guedalla (1927), and also as an appendix to M & B v, 531-60.

Aristocracy

I am not disposed for a moment to admit that my pedigree is not as good as that of the Cavendishes.

MD 212

Their table talk is stable talk.

Ibid

'Ancient lineage,' said Millbank, 'I never heard of a peer with ancient lineage. The real old families of this country are to be found among the peasantry.'

Coningsby bk iii, ch 4

We owe the English peerage to three sources: the spoliation of the Church; the open and flagrant sale of honours by the elder Stuarts; and the borough-mongering of our own time.

Ibid

The House of Commons is a more aristocratic body than the House of Lords. The fact is that a great peer would be a greater man now in the House of Commons than in the House of Lords. Nobody wants a second chamber except a few disreputable individuals.

Ibid

There is no title in the world for which I have such contempt as that of a baronet.

[Hatton] Sybil bk iv, ch 7

An aristocracy hesitates before it yields its confidence but never does so grudgingly.

LGB 318

An aristocracy is rather apt to exaggerate the qualities and magnify the importance of a plebeian leader.

Ibid

The first duty of an aristocracy is to lead, to guide, and to enlighten; to soften vulgar prejudices and to dare to encounter popular passion.

LGB 325

As property has its duties as well as its rights, rank has its bores as well as its pleasures.

Sybil bk ii, ch 11

The feudal system may have worn out, but its main principle, that the tenure of property should be the fulfilment of duty, is the essence of good government.

Lothair, general preface

A feeling of satiety, almost inseparable from large possessions, is a surer cause of misery than ungratified desires.

Lothair ch 25

The palace is not safe when the cottage is not happy.

B 556

England

'Two nations between whom there is no intercourse and no sympathy; who are as ignorant of each other's habits, thoughts and feelings as if they were dwellers in different zones or inhabitants of different planets; who are formed by a different breeding, are fed by a different food, are ordered by different manners, and are not governed by the same laws.'

'You speak of –' said Egremont, hesitatingly.

'THE RICH AND THE POOR.'

Sybil bk ii, ch 5

If we could only so contrive our lives as to go into the country for the first note of the nightingale and return to town for the first note of the muffin bell, existence, it is to be humbly presumed, might be more enjoyable.

Lothair ch 9

When the passions of the English, naturally an enthusiastic people, are excited on a subject of finance, their will, their determination and resource are irresistible.

Endymion ch 78

England is the only country which, when it enters into a quarrel that it believes to be just never ceases its efforts till it has achieved its aim.

M & B iv, 310

I was told that the Privileged and the People formed Two Nations.

[*Egremont*] *Sybil* bk iv, ch 8

England is the only important European community that is still governed by traditionary interests.

LGB 555

London is a roost for every bird.

Lothair ch 11

London is a nation not a city.

Lothair ch 27

The salvation of Europe is the affair of a past generation. We want something else now. The salvation of England should be the subject, rather, of our present thoughts.

Endymion ch 1

In England when a new character appears in our circles the first question always is, 'Who is he?' In France it is, 'What is he?' In England, 'How much a year? In France, 'What has he done?'

Coningsby bk v, ch 11

London is a nation not a city; with a population greater than some kingdoms, and districts as different as if they were under different governments and spoke different languages.

Lothair ch 27

London is a modern Babylon.

Tancred bk v, ch 5

Infanticide is practised as extensively and as legally in England as it is on the banks of the Ganges; a circumstance which apparently has not yet engaged the attention of the Society for the Propagation of the Gospel in Foreign Parts.

Sybil bk ii, ch 10

An insular country, subject to fogs, and with a powerful middle class, requires grave statesmen.

Endymion ch 37

England is unrivalled for two things – sport and politics.

Coningsby bk ii, ch 1

Gastronomy

Thank God for something warm at last [of champagne arriving with the pudding after a series of ill-heated courses at a public dinner].

Attrib.

The still hissing bacon and eggs that looked like tufts of primroses.

Coningsby bk iii, ch 1

'They say primroses make a capital salad,' said Lord St Jerome. 'Barbarian,' exclaimed Lady St Jerome, 'I see you want luncheon.'

Lothair ch 13

'I rather like bad wine,' said Mr Mountchesney; 'one gets so bored with good wine.'

Sybil bk i, ch 1

Turbots visiting trout are patricians visiting country cousins [of an exchange of fish presents].

B 417

The rosy-coloured tribute of Torbay [of a basket of prawns].

Ibid

A good eater must be a good man; for a good eater must have a good digestion, and a good digestion depends upon a good conscience.

Young Duke bk i, ch 14

A dinner of wits is proverbially a palace of silence.

Endymion ch 91

It was a lively dinner. Lord St Jerome loved conversation, though he never conversed. 'There must be an audience,' he would say, 'and I am the audience.'

Lothair ch 9

Lord Monmouth's dinners at Paris were celebrated … What was the secret of his success? The simplest in the world, though no one seemed aware of it. His Lordship's plates were always hot.

Coningsby bk vi, ch 2

I feel quite embarrassed but forget my embarrassment in the exquisite flavour. All this because I once mentioned my detestation of hosts who give you inferior claret at dinner when alone sensible men drink wine, and reserve their superior *crus* till after the repast [offered 'Grand Château Margaux 1870' at Hatfield, alone of those at table, his host being absent].

B 711

A gentle dallying with a whiting, that chicken of the ocean.

Young Duke bk iii, ch 7

All paradise opens! Let me die eating ortolans to the sound of soft music.

Young Duke bk i, ch 10

On the whole I prefer the perfume of fruit even to that of flowers. It is more mystical and thrilling; more rapturous.

R 94

Himself

I do not care to be amused – I prefer to be interested.

MD 37

I think to talk well is a rare gift – quite as rare as singing; and yet you expect everyone to be able to talk and very few to be able to sing.

MD 38

I am never well, save in action, and then I am immortal.

MD 47

I want to be Prime Minister [asked by Lord Melbourne in 1834 'Now tell me what you want to be'].

W.M. Torrens, *Memoirs ... of Viscount Melbourne* 275

I never deny; I never contradict; I sometimes forget [of his relations with Queen Victoria].

Elizabeth Longford, *Victoria R.I.* 403

To become a K.G. with a Cecil is something for a Disraeli.

Victoria R.I. 415

You have heard me called a flatterer and it is true.
Everyone likes flattery and when you come to Royalty, you should lay it on with a trowel [to Matthew Arnold].

M & B vi, 463

I love the Queen – perhaps the only person in this world left to me that I do love.

M & B vi, 462

I will not go down to posterity talking bad grammar [when correcting the proofs of his last parliamentary speech, 31 March 1881].

> M & B vi, 612

Power! It has come to me too late. There were days, when on waking I felt I could move dynasties and governments, but that has passed away [on becoming Prime Minister in 1868].

> M & B v, 299

Yes, I have climbed to the top of the greasy pole [on the same occasion].

> DD 52

My mind is a revolutionary mind. It is a continental mind. I am only great in action. If ever I am placed in a truly eminent position I shall prove this.

> [From 'the Mutilated Diary', 1833] M & B i, 236

Poetry is the safeguard of my passions, but I wish to act what I write.

> M & B v, 301

I always shrink from any expression of political sentimentalism.

> M & B iv, 337

But you must stick to Northcote. He represents the respectability of the party. I wholly sympathize with you because I was never respectable myself.

> B 729

The Jews & Jerusalem

If the Jews had not prevailed upon the Romans to crucify
our Lord, what would have become of the Atonement?

LGB 488

Could that be a crime [the Crucifixion] which secured for
all mankind eternal joy? Which vanquished Satan and
opened the gates of Paradise?

LGB 488

The world has discovered by this time that it is impossible
to destroy the Jews.

LGB 494

They [the Jews] are a living and most striking evidence of
the falsity of that pernicious doctrine of modern times, the
natural equality of man.

LGB 496

... all the tendencies of the Jewish race are conservative.
Their bias is to religion, property, and natural aristocracy.

LGB 497

But existing society has chosen to persecute this race which
should furnish its choice allies. And what have been the
consequences? ... the persecution of the Jewish race has
deprived European society of an important conservative
element and added to the destructive party an influential
ally.

LGB 497-9

But Babylon has vanished and Jerusalem remains, and what are the waters of the Euphrates to the brook of Kedron!

LGB 505

Christians may continue to persecute Jews, and Jews may persist in disbelieving Christianity, but who can deny that Jesus Christ, the incarnate son of the Most High God, is the eternal glory of the Jewish race?

LGB 507

Christianity is completed Judaism or it is nothing. Christianity is incomprehensible without Judaism as Judaism is incomplete without Christianity.

Sybil bk ii, ch 12

Jerusalem at midday in midsummer is a city of stone in a land of iron with a sky of brass.

Tancred bk iii, ch 3

'The Arabs are only Jews upon horseback,' said Baroni.

Tancred bk iv, ch 3

I look upon the Church as the only Jewish institution remaining … The Jews owe everything to the Church and are fools to oppose it.

R 103

I come from a race which never forgives an injury nor forgets a benefit.

B 706

It is no longer difficult to reach Jerusalem; the real difficulty is the one experienced by the crusaders; to know what to do when you have arrived there.

Tancred bk ii, ch 11

Literature & History

When I want to read a novel I write one.

M & B vi, 636

There is no reason to doubt the story which represents him as using more than once in conversation with Her Majesty on literary subjects the words: 'We authors, Ma'am.'

M & B v, 49

She is an excellent creature, but she can never remember which came first, the Greeks or the Romans [of Mrs Disraeli].

G.W.E. Russell, *Collections and Recollections* ch 1

Your Majesty is the head of the literary profession.

Ibid ch 23

Read no history, nothing but biography, for that is life without theory.

Contarini Fleming pt i, ch 23

You know who the critics are? The men who have failed in literature and art.

[*Mr Phoebus*] *Lothair* ch 35

I may say of our literature that it has one characteristic which distinguishes it from almost all the other literatures of modern Europe, and that is its exuberant productiveness.

Royal Literary Fund Dinner, 6 May 1868

Assassination has never changed the course of history.
H of C, 1 May 1865

An author who talks about his own books is almost as bad as a mother who talks about her own children.
Glasgow, 19 November 1873

Some poets who would be quite forgotten live, and live vigorously by a single line. 'Fine by degrees and beautifully less' is an example.

R 97

Books are companions even if you don't open them.
Z ii, 186

I have a passion for books and trees. I like to look at them.
R 130

The most philosophical of bigots and the most poetical of prose writers [Southey].
Vivian Grey bk iv, ch 1

Books are fatal; they are the curse of the human race. Nine-tenths of existing books are nonsense and the clever books are the refutation of that nonsense.
[*Mr Phoebus*] *Lothair* ch 29

Guanoed her mind by reading French novels.
Tancred bk ii, ch 9

The greatest stretch of intellect in the world is to write a first-rate work of fiction.

B 732

Mr Wordy's History of the Late War in twenty volumes, a
capital work which proves that Providence was on the side
of the Tories.

[Rigby] Coningsby bk iii, ch 2

All the great things have been done by little nations. It is
the Jordan and the Ilyssus which have civilized the modern
races.

Tancred bk iii, ch 7

They revenged themselves on tyranny by destroying
civilization [of the Albanians].

Contarini Fleming pt v, ch 12

Love & Marriage

Tobacco is the tomb of love.

Sybil bk ii, ch 16

It destroys one's nerves to be amiable every day to the same human being.

Young Duke bk iii, ch 2

I have often thought that every woman should marry and no man ... [But] I would not answer for myself if I could find an affectionate family with good shooting and first-rate claret.

[*Hugo Bohun*] *Lothair* ch 30

The only useless life is women's.

[*Lucretia*] *Coningsby* bk iv, ch 15

Feminine vanity, that divine gift which makes women charming.

Tancred bk ii, ch 8

'George, there is one word in the English language of which you are ignorant.' 'What is that?' 'Gratitude, George.' [to George Smythe, who wondered at the success of his marriage].

Sir William Gregory, *Autobiography* 94

Man is a predatory animal. The worthiest objects of his chase are women and power. After I married Mary Anne I desisted from the one and devoted my life to the pursuit of the other.

MD 95

I am one of those people who feel much more deeply than I
ever express.

MD 96

My nature demands that my life should be perpetual love
[letter to Mary Anne].

B 771

Why you are more like a mistress than a wife [returning to
supper of a pie from Fortnum & Mason and a bottle of
champagne].

B 467

There are two powers at which men should never grumble
– the weather and their wives.

MD 29

A female friend amiable, clever, and devoted is a
possession more valuable than parks and palaces.

MD 51

There is no love but love at first sight.

Henrietta Temple bk ii, ch 4

The most severe of critics but – a perfect wife. [Dedication
to Mary Anne]

Sybil

We were so delighted, Mrs Disraeli and I, that after we got
home we actually danced a jig (or was it a hornpipe?) in
our bedroom [after a notable success in Edinburgh].

M & B iv, 559

Grosvenor Gate [their London house] has become a hospital, but a hospital with you is worth a palace with anybody else [to Mary Anne when they were confined by illness to their bedrooms].

M & B iv, 572

This is a dismal business: it always depresses me. After a funeral I am cheerful. I feel that one has got rid of someone [coming away from a wedding].

DD 460

She rules her husband, but that I suppose is always the case when marriages are what is called happy [of Lady Lytton].

Z ii, 285

Maxims

Lectures are grains of mustard seed.

Falconet ch 8

I never trust a gentleman by halves.

DD 497

Knowledge of mankind is knowledge of their passions.

Young Duke bk i, ch 2

As a general rule no one has money who ought to have it.

Endymion ch 65

Adventures are to the adventurous.

Coningsby bk iii, ch 1

A precedent embalms a principle.

H of C, 22 February 1848

Justice is truth in action.

H of C, 11 February 1851

This shows how much easier it is to be critical than correct.

H of C, 24 January 1860

Man is only truly great when he acts from the passions.

Coningsby bk iii, ch 1

Little things affect little minds.

Sybil bk iii, ch 2

All is race; there is no other truth.

Tancred bk ii, ch 14

The East is a career.

Ibid

I hate definitions.

Vivian Grey bk ii, ch 6

No one likes his dependants to be treated with respect, for such treatment forms an unpleasant contrast to his own conduct.

Ibid bk iii, ch 7

Experience is the child of thought and thought is the child of action. We cannot learn men from books.

Ibid bk v, ch 1

There is moderation even in excess.

Ibid bk vi, ch 1

If you wish to win a man's heart allow him to confute you.

Ibid bk ii, ch 14

Variety is the mother of Enjoyment.

Ibid bk v, ch 4

Man is not the creature of circumstances. Circumstances are the creature of man.

Ibid bk vi, ch 7

Eloquence is the child of Knowledge.

The Young Duke bk v, ch 6

Success is the child of Audacity.

Rise of Iskander ch 4

Silence is the mother of Truth.

Tancred bk iv, ch 4

He who laughs at Destiny will gain Fortune.

Ixion in Heaven pt 1, ch 8

Thought is often bolder than speech.

Ixion pt ii, ch 3

To be conscious that you are ignorant is a great step to knowledge.

Sybil bk i, ch 5

There is no wisdom like frankness.

Sybil bk iv, ch 9

Feeble deeds are vainer far than words.

Ibid bk v, ch 3

Never take anything for granted.

Salthill, 5 October 1864

What we anticipate seldom occurs; what we least expected generally happens.

Henrietta Temple bk ii, ch 4

To govern men you must either excel them in their accomplishments or despise them.

M & B i, 154-5

Debt is the prolific mother of folly and crime.

Henrietta Temple bk ii, ch 1

Truth in general must be commonplace or it would not be true.

Henrietta Temple bk vi, ch 24

Men were made to listen as well as to talk ... Nature has given us two ears but only one mouth.

[*Count Mirabel*] *Henrietta Temple* bk vi, ch 24

To believe in the heroic makes heroes.

[*Sidonia*] *Coningsby* bk iii, ch 1

Parliament

What by way of jest they call the Lower House.

Coningsby bk iii, ch 4

Though I sit down now, the time will come when you will hear me.

Maiden Speech, H of C, 7 December 1837

I am dead, dead but in the Elysian Fields [on becoming a peer].

M & B v, 49

Between ourselves I could floor them all. This *entre nous*. I was never more confident of anything than that I could carry everything before me in that House. The time will come.

Letters to His Sister, 7 February 1833

A man may speak very well in the House of Commons and fail very completely in the House of Lords. There are two distinct styles requisite. I intend ... to give a specimen of both: in the Lower House 'Don Juan' may perhaps be our model, in the Upper House 'Paradise Lost'.

Young Duke bk v, ch 6

The House of Commons is absolute. It is the State. 'L'Etat c'est moi.'

[*Oswald Millbank*] *Coningsby* bk vii, ch 2

Never complain and never explain [of attacks in Parliament].

Quoted J. Morley, *Gladstone* i, 123

Parliamentary speaking, like playing the fiddle, requires practice.

> H of C, 13 July 1871

I look upon Parliamentary Government as the noblest government in the world.

> Manchester, 3 April 1872

All the best speakers in the House of Commons are after-dinner speakers.

> H of C, 4 April 1851

I look upon the House of Commons as a mere vestry. Reform has dished it.

> [*Waldershare*] *Endymion* ch 40

The Lords do not encourage wit, and so are obliged to put up with pertness.

> *Young Duke* bk i, ch 6

Divisions in the House of Lords nowadays are so thinly scattered that, when one occurs, the peers cackle as if they had laid an egg.

> *Tancred* bk ii, ch 5

Your last word was re-vo-lut-i-on [when Gladstone seemed to have lost his thread in a speech].

> DG 26

When Gentlemen cease to be returned to Parliament this Empire will perish.

> DD 461

He'll do [of Lord Hartington who yawned during his own maiden speech].

> DD 450

For twelve years this man was a bore: he has suddenly become an institution [of a Member who had recently acquired notoriety].

DD 403

If this man had eyes, how the House would damn them [of a Member ever raising and lowering his eye-glass].

DD 404

The greatest opportunity that can be offered to an Englishman – a seat in the House of Commons.

Endymion ch 72

In the history of this country the depository of power is always unpopular; all combine against it; it always falls.

[*Sidonia*] *Coningsby* bk iv, ch 13

I read this morning an awful, though monotonous, manifesto in the great organ of public opinion [*The Times*], which always makes me tremble: Olympian bolts; and yet I could not help fancying amid their rumbling terrors I heard the plaintive treble of the Treasury Bench.

H of C, 13 February 1851

No Government can be long secure without a formidable Opposition.

Coningsby bk ii, ch 1

I admit the immense difficulty of encountering any argument that is based on 'unconstitutional' objections. I never yet have found any definition of what that epithet means, and I believe that, with the single exception of the word 'un-English', it baffles discussion more than any other in our language.

H of C, 26 April 1858

A series of congratulatory regrets [Hartington's Resolution on the Berlin Treaty].

Knightsbridge, 27 July 1878

As for our majority ... one is enough.

Endymion ch 64

If anything can get the nonsense out of man it is the House of Commons.

[*Lord Bartram*] *Endymion* ch 5

The greatest compliment you can pay to a woman is to give her your time, and it is the same with our Senate. A man who is always in his place becomes a sort of favourite.

Ibid

The old gentleman-like times when members of Parliament had nobody to please and Ministers of State nothing to do.

[*Mr Berners*] *Sybil* bk v, ch 1

Pretending that people can be better off than they are is radicalism and nothing else.

[*The Warwickshire peer*] *Ibid*

Unless you are always there, how can you lead the House of Commons? How can you feel their pulse? How can you know the men?

M & B v, 500

I do not dread the political future as regards the electors of England. I wish I could say the same of Scotland and Ireland.

DD 468

This is a measure of Necessity conceived in a spirit of Conciliation.

DD 496-7

A parliamentary career, that old superstition of the eighteenth century, was important when there was no other source of power or fame.

Tancred bk ii, ch. 13

Parliament seems to me the very place which a man of action should avoid ... in this age it is not Parliament which does the real work.

Ibid

People

Take care of that man! He means what he says [Bismarck].

M & B iv, 341

The lawyer has spoilt the statesman [Lord Brougham].

Vivian Grey bk v, ch 6

Under his influence [Gladstone's] we have legalized confiscation, consecrated sacrilege, condoned high treason.

H of C, 27 February 1871

A sophisticated rhetorician inebriated by the exuberance of his own verbosity [Gladstone].

Knightsbridge, 27 July 1878

Joseph Toplady Falconet [i.e. Gladstone] was essentially a prig, and among prigs there is a freemasonry that never fails. All the prigs spoke of him as the coming man.

Falconet ch 5

Posterity will do justice to that unprincipled maniac Gladstone – extraordinary mixture of envy, vindictiveness, hypocrisy and superstition; and with one commanding characteristic – whether Prime Minister or Leader of the Opposition, whether preaching, praying, speechifying or scribbling – never a gentleman.

M & B vi, 67

Easy to say he is mad. It looks like it. My theory about him is unchanged: a ceaseless Tartuffe from the beginning. That sort of man does not go mad at 70 [Gladstone].

M & B vi, 181

The transient and embarrassed phantom of Lord Goderich.

Endymion ch 3

The Arch-Mediocrity who presided, rather than ruled, over this Cabinet of Mediocrities [Lord Liverpool].

Coningsby bk ii, ch 1

He has no sympathy with the past, no respect for tradition; he has confidence in his own infallibility [Robert Lowe].

Newport Pagnell, 5 February 1874

There is nothing that he likes and almost everything that he hates [Robert Lowe].

H of C, 3 April 1868

He seems to think that posterity is a pack-horse always ready to be loaded [Palmerston].

H of C, 3 June 1862

Peel ... guarded his aspirates with immense care. I have known him slip. The correctness was not spontaneous. He had managed his elocution like his temper: neither was originally good.

CP 18

A transcendent administrator of public business and a matchless master of debate in a public assembly [Peel].

LGB 304

Sir Robert Peel had a great deficiency; he was without imagination. Wanting imagination he lacked prescience ... His judgement was faultless provided he had not to deal with the future.

LGB 304-5

The greatest member of parliament that ever lived [Peel].

LGB 319-20

The Rt. Hon. Gentleman caught the Whigs bathing and ran away with their clothes [Peel].

H of C, 28 February 1845

He traces the steam engine always back to the tea kettle [Peel].

H of C, 11 April 1845

We have a great Parliamentary middleman. It is well known what a middleman is; he is a man who bamboozles one party and plunders the other [Peel].

H of C, 11 April 1845

He is a burglar of others' intellect … There is no statesman who has committed political petty larceny on so great a scale [Peel].

M & B ii, 385

He embalmed no great political truth in immortal words. His flights were ponderous; he soared with the wing of the vulture rather than the plume of the eagle [Peel].

LGB 314

'Frank and explicit' – that is the right line to take when you wish to conceal your own mind and to confuse the minds of others ['The Gentleman in Downing Street', i.e. Peel].

Sybil bk vi, ch 1

He is a great master of gibes and flouts and jeers [The 3rd Marquis of Salisbury].

H of C, 5 August 1874

Lord Salisbury and myself have brought you back peace – but a peace I hope with honour.

H of C, 16 July 1878

The noble Lord is the Rupert of Parliamentary discussion [Lord Stanley, later 14th Earl of Derby].

H of C, 24 April 1844

It is a dazzling adventure for the House of Stanley [rumoured offer of the Crown of Greece] ... but they are not an imaginative race and, I fancy, will prefer Knowsley to the Parthenon and Lancashire to the Attic plain.

DGT 47

I do not know that there is anything which excites enthusiasm in him except when he contemplates the surrender of some national policy [The 15th Earl of Derby].

H of L, 5 March 1881

He has been called fortunate but fortune is a divinity which has never favoured those who are not at the same time sagacious and intrepid, inventive and patient [The Duke of Wellington].

H of C, 15 November 1852

The Duke of Wellington has left to his country a greater legacy even than his fame: he has left to them the contemplation of his character.

H of C, 15 November 1852

It was clear that the energies which had twice entered Paris as a conqueror ... would not be content to subside into ermined insignificance [Wellington].

Sybil bk i, ch 3

He has yet to learn that petulance is not sarcasm and that insolence is not invective [Sir Charles Wood].

H of C, 16 December 1852

Phrases & Opinions

The sweet simplicity of the three per cents.

Endymion ch 96

I grew intoxicated with my own eloquence.

Contarini Fleming pt i, ch 7

I believe that they went out like all good things with the Stuarts [*Waldershare* on a 'pottle of strawberries'].

Endymion ch 99

He was not an intellectual Croesus, but his pocket was lined with sixpences.

Lothair ch 28

A public man of light and leading.

Sybil bk v, ch 1

Sanitas sanitatum omnia sanitas.

Manchester, 3 April 1872

The Egremonts had never said anything that could be remembered or done anything that could be recalled.

Sybil bk i, ch 3

Mr Kremlin was distinguished for ignorance for he had only one idea – and that was wrong.

Sybil bk iv, ch 5

Like all great travellers I have seen more than I remember, and remember more than I have seen.

[*Essper*] *Vivian Grey* bk viii, ch 4

The frigid theories of a generalising age.

Coningsby bk ix, ch 7

He was fresh and full of faith that 'something would turn up'.

[Fakredeen] Tancred bk iii, ch 6

Men moralise among ruins.

Tancred bk v, ch 5

Progress to what and from where ... The European talks of progress because by an ingenious application of some scientific acquirements he has established a society which has mistaken comfort for civilization.

Tancred bk iii, ch 7

The morning air is refreshing when one has lost one's money.

Lothair ch 29

There are amusing people who do not interest and interesting people who do not amuse.

Lothair ch 41

Potatoes at this moment, Madam [to a lady, at dinner, who wanted action against Russia and asked him what he was waiting for].

MD 222

Of what use is my coronet to me, my dear Lady, so long as Sir John Sebright is alive [to Lady Sebright who apologised for addressing him as 'Mr Disraeli'].

Ibid

There are three kinds of lies: lies, damned lies and statistics.

Attrib. by Mark Twain, *Autobiography* vol i, 246

The Statistical Conference, a body of men who, for their hideousness, the ladies declare, were never equalled.

M & B iv, 282

My butler is a pompous booby.

M & B iv, 572

The once firm guardians of popular rights simper in the enervating atmosphere of gilded saloons [of the Press, especially Delane, Editor of *The Times* in May 1858].

B 381

I prophesy as becomes one in the sunset of life – or rather I sh'd say the twilight of existence [May 1880].

B 722

A missive of menacing hospitality [from Lord Beauchamp].

Z ii, 273

Except at Wycombe Fair in my youth I have never seen anything so bad as *Pinafore*.

Z ii, 180

The gardener like all head-gardeners was opinionated.

Lothair ch 13

Every man has a right to be conceited till he is successful.

'Advertisement' to *The Young Duke*

We should never lose an occasion. Opportunity is more powerful even than conquerors and prophets.

Tancred bk v ch 5

The fate of a nation will ultimately depend on the strength and health of the population.

Lothair ch 29

Nothing like mamma's darling for upsetting the coach.

Tancred bk i ch 3

A forest is like the ocean, monotonous only to the ignorant. It is a life of ceaseless variety.

Reminiscences 118

It was a melancholy day for human nature when that stupid Lord Anson, after beating about for three years, found himself again at Greenwich. The circumnavigation of our world was accomplished, but the illimitable was annihilated and a fatal blow [dealt] to all imagination.

Reminiscences 88

Lord Shelburne used to say that perfect society was wives without husbands and husbands without wives.

Reminiscences 87

It will generally be found that all great political questions end in the tenure of land.

Reminiscences 74

Politics

Protection is not a principle, but an expedient.

H of C, 17 March 1845

A Conservative Government is an organised hypocrisy.

H of C, 17 March 1845

England does not love coalitions.

H of C, 16 December 1852

Finality is not the language of politics.

H of C, 28 February 1859

To put an end to these bloated armaments.

H of C, 8 May 1862

You are not going, I hope, to leave the destinies of the British Empire to prigs and pedants.

H of C, 5 February 1863

Party is organised opinion.

Oxford, 25 November 1864

Change is inevitable. In a progressive country change is constant.

Edinburgh, 29 October 1867

I had to prepare the mind of the country, and to educate – if it be not arrogant to use such a phrase – educate our party [on the Reform Act of 1867].

Edinburgh, 29 October 1867

I believe that without party Parliamentary government is impossible.

Manchester, 3 April 1872

As I sat opposite the Treasury Bench the ministers reminded me of one of those marine landscapes not very unusual on the coasts of South America. You behold a range of exhausted volcanoes.

Manchester, 3 April 1872

King Louis Philippe once said to me that he attributed the great success of the British nation in political life to their talking politics after dinner.

Glasgow, 19 November 1873

One of the greatest of Romans when asked what were his politics replied, *Imperium et Libertas*. That would not make a bad programme for a British Ministry.

Mansion House, 10 November 1879

Damn your principles! Stick to your party [reply to Bulwer Lytton].

Attrib. Latham, *Famous Sayings*

The strange vicissitudes of political life.

LGB

Protection is not only dead but damned.

M & B iii, 241

In the *Town* yesterday as I am told, 'Some one asked Disraeli, in offering himself for Marylebone on what he intended *to stand* – "On my head" was the reply.'

Letters to his Sister 119

Tadpole and Taper were great friends. Neither of them ever despaired of the Commonwealth.

Coningsby bk i, ch 1

Conservatism discards Prescription, shrinks from Principle, disavows Progress; having rejected all respect for antiquity, it offers no redress for the present, and makes no preparation for the future.

Coningsby bk ii, ch 5

'A sound Conservative government,' said Taper musingly. 'I understand: Tory men and Whig measures.'

Coningsby bk ii, ch 6

It seems to me a barren thing this Conservatism – an unhappy cross-breed, the mule of politics that engenders nothing.

Coningsby bk iii, ch 5

The practice of politics in the East may be defined by one word – dissimulation.

Contarini Fleming pt v, ch 10

That fatal drollery called a representative government.

Tancred bk ii, ch 13

A majority is always the best repartee.

Tancred bk ii, ch 14

Nothing is more ruinous to political connection than the fear of justly rewarding your friends … It is not becoming in any Minister to decry party who has risen by party. We should always remember that if we were not partisans we should not be Ministers.

B 389

Patronage is the outward and visible sign of an inward and spiritual grace, and that is Power.

B 388

There is no act of treachery or meanness of which a political party is not capable; for in politics there is no honour.

[*Cleveland*] *Vivian Grey* bk iv, ch 1

There was indeed a considerable shouting about what they called Conservative principles; but the awkward question naturally arose, what will you conserve?

Coningsby bk ii, ch 5

I have promised many a peerage without committing myself, by an ingenious habit of deference, which cannot be mistaken by the future noble.

[*Taper*] *Coningsby* bk ii, ch 6

It is the personal that interests mankind, that fires their imagination, and wins their hearts.

Coningsby bk ii, ch 7

This party treats institutions as we do our pheasants, they preserve only to destroy them [of the Conservatives].

Coningsby bk iii, ch 5

I have ever been of the opinion that revolutions are not to be evaded.

[*Sidonia*] *Coningsby* bk iv, ch 11

Of this I am convinced myself, that bribery and corruption affect very little the course of public affairs.

H of C, 30 May 1867

Thus you have a starving population, an absentee aristocracy, and an alien Church, and in addition the weakest executive in the world. That is the Irish Question.

H of C, 16 February 1844

In politics experiments mean revolutions.

Popanilla ch 4

The Key of India is London.

H of L, 5 March 1881

The hare-brained chatter of irresponsible frivolity.

Guildhall, 9 November 1878

The programme of the Conservative party is to maintain the Constitution of the country.

Manchester, 3 April 1872

The grovelling tyranny of self-government.

Tancred bk vi, ch 3

The truth is progress and reaction are but words to mystify the millions. They mean nothing, they are nothing, they are phrases and not facts.

LGB 331

The movement of the middle classes for the abolition of slavery was virtuous, but it was not wise.

LGB 324

Strange that a manufacture which charms infancy and soothes old age should so frequently occasion political disaster [of sugar].

LGB 322

I have always considered that the Tory party was the
national party of England.

Edinburgh, 26 October 1867

I repeat that all power is a trust and that we are accountable
for its exercise; that from the people and for the people, all
springs and all must exist.

Vivian Grey ch 7

The world is wearied of statesmen whom democracy has
degraded into politicians.

Lothair ch 17

An obsolete oligarchy [the Whigs].

DD 471

Look to Lord Roehampton; he is the man. He does not care
a rush whether the revenue increases or declines. He is
thinking of real politics: foreign affairs; maintaining our
power in Europe.

Endymion ch 64

The very phrase 'foreign affairs' makes an Englishman
convinced that I am about to treat of subjects with which
he has no concern.

Manchester, 3 April 1872

To pretend that you can assist and support the commerce
of this country by commercial treaties is a mere delusion.

M & B iv, 314

I don't know any member of this House … who has ever
maintained the monstrous proposition that England ought
never under any circumstances to interfere in the affairs of
foreign states.

M & B iv, 315-16

France is a Kingdom with a Republic for its capital.

Coningsby bk v, ch 11

The pendulum swings.

DD 445

Religion

The Church of England is not a mere depositary of doctrine. The Church of England is a part of England – it is a part of our strength and a part of our liberties, a part of our national character.

H of C, 27 February 1861

'What is Church and State?' said Venetia. 'As good things as strawberries and cream,' said the Doctor, laughing, 'and like them always best united.'

Venetia bk i, ch 9

Man is a being born to believe.

Oxford, 25 November 1864

Is man an ape or an angel? Now I am on the side of the angels.

Ibid

I hold that the characteristic of the present age is craving credulity.

Ibid

I am the blank page between the Old and the New Testament [alleged to have been said to Queen Victoria].

B 504

His Christianity was muscular.

Endymion ch 3

The Athanasian Creed is the most splendid ecclesiastical
lyric ever poured forth by the genius of man.

Endymion ch 54

In a truly religious [sc. Catholic] family there would always
be a Father Coleman or a Monsignore Catesby to guide and
to instruct. But a Protestant, if he wants aid or advice on
any matter, can only go to his solicitor.

Lothair ch 18

Pray remember, Mr Dean, no dogma, no Dean.

M & B iv, 368

The spiritual nature of man is stronger than codes or
constitutions. No government can exist which does not
recognise that for its foundation, and no legislation last
which does not flow from that fountain.

Glasgow, 19 November 1872

Where can we find faith in a nation of sectaries?

Coningsby bk iv, ch 13

The Church is a sacred corporation for the promulgation ...
in Europe of certain Asian principles which, although local
in their birth, are of divine original and eternal application.

Coningsby, preface to 5th edition

The Church of Rome is to be respected as the only
Hebraeo-Christian Church extant.

Sybil bk ii, ch 12

What the soul is to the man the Church is to the world.

[*Cardinal Grandison*] *Lothair* ch 17

You can't fight for a person you don't know [of Episcopal
candidates].

M & B v, 69

Ecclesiastical affairs rage here [Balmoral]. Send me
Crockford's Directory. I must be armed.

Ibid

There is in his idiosyncracy a strange fund of enthusiasm, a
quality which ought never to be possessed by an
Archbishop of Canterbury or a Prime Minister of England
[of Bishop Tait].

B 510

The head of the house [an Oxford College] of which Gaston
had become a member was one of those distinguished
divines who do not believe in divinity.

Falconet ch 1

I thought the Lord's Prayer a masterpiece. It was the most
perfect exponent of the purest religious feeling that has
ever appeared. And while it soothed the cottage, it was
difficult to conceive a society so refined that it would not
satisfy.

R 102

I don't like Bishops; I think there is no use in them.

[Lord St Aldegonde] Lothair ch 47

Society & Sport

Don't talk too much at present; do not *try* to talk. But whenever you speak, speak with self-assurance. Speak in a subdued tone and always look at the person you are addressing.

Contarini Fleming pt i, ch 23

Never argue. In society nothing must be discussed; give only results. If any person differs from you, bow and turn the conversation. In society never think; always be on the watch.

Ibid

There is no doubt that that great pummice-stone, society, smooths down the edges of your thoughts and manners.

Young Duke bk iv, ch 3

Christianity teaches us to love our neighbour as ourself; modern society acknowledges no neighbour.

Sybil bk ii, ch 5

Be amusing. Never tell unkind stories; above all never tell long ones.

MD 203

The two thousand Brahmins who constitute the World [of society].

Young Duke bk iii, ch 4

My idea of an agreeable person is a person who agrees with me.

[*Hugo Bohun*] *Lothair* ch 41

There are no fits of caprice so hasty and so violent as those of society. Society is indeed all passion and no heart.

Venetia bk iv, ch 18

[Society] instils into us that indefinable tact seldom obtained in later life, which prevents us from saying the wrong thing, and often inspires us to do the right.

WW 323

You are yet too young to comprehend how much in life depends upon manner. Whenever you see a man who is successful in society try to discover what makes him pleasing and if possible adopt his system.

Contarini Fleming pt i, ch 23

What can one expect of a government which does not move in society.

DG 17

Talk to women, talk to women as much as you can. This is the best school. This is the way to gain fluency, because you need not care what you say, and had better not be sensible.

Contarini Fleming pt i, ch 23

Society and politics have much to do with each other but they are not identical.

Endymion ch 44

However vast may appear the world in which we move, we all of us live in a limited circle.

Endymion ch 80

To 'throw over' a host is the most heinous of all social crimes. It ought never to be pardoned.

Lothair ch 27

Nonchalance is the *métier* of your modern hostess; and so long as the house is not on fire or the furniture kicked, you may be even ignorant who is the priestess of the hospitable fane in which you worship.

Young Duke bk ii, ch 9

Lady St Jerome received Lothair, as Pinto said, with extreme unction.

Lothair ch 28

In England personal distinction is the only passport to the society of the great.

Vivian Grey bk i, ch 7

A smile for a friend, and a sneer for the world, is the way to govern mankind, and such was the motto of Vivian Grey.

Vivian Grey bk i, ch 3

To render the romantic simplicity complete Lady Londonderry, in a colossal conservatory, condescended to make tea from a suite of golden pots and kettles.

R 36

We all of us live too much in a circle.

Sybil bk iii, ch 6

Woman alone can organise a drawing-room; man succeeds sometimes in a library.

Coningsby bk iii, ch 2

Those mysterious characters [jockeys], who with their influence over their superiors and their total want of sympathy with their species are our only match for the oriental eunuch.

Young Duke bk i, ch 2

A *dark* horse, which had never been thought of and which the careless St James had never even observed in the list, rushed past the grandstand in sweeping triumph.

Young Duke bk ii, ch 5

'You do not know what the Derby is?' he [Bentinck] moaned out. 'Yes I do; it is the blue ribbon of the turf.'

LGB 539

A canter is a cure for every ill.

Young Duke bk ii, ch 11

Tact teaches you to be silent. Inquirers who are always inquiring never learn anything.

Endymion ch 61

Every day when he looked into the glass and gave the last touch to his exquisite toilette he offered grateful thanks to Providence that his family was not unworthy of him.

['*The Duke*'] *Lothair* ch 1

Printing has destroyed education. The essence of education is the education of the body. What I admire in the order to which you belong [the aristocracy] is that they live in the air; that they excel in athletic sports; that they can only speak one language; and that they never read.

[*Mr Phoebus*] *Lothair* ch 29

Tradesmen nowadays console themselves for not getting their bills paid by asking their customers to dinner.

Young Duke bk iii, ch 8

The age of chivalry is past. Bores have succeeded to dragons.

Young Duke bk ii, ch 5

Youth & Age

Both had exhausted life in their teens, and all that remained for them was to mourn, amid the ruins of their reminiscences, over the extinction of excitement.

Sybil bk i, ch 1

'Nothing can do me good,' said Alfred, throwing away his almost untasted peach; 'I should be quite content if anything could do me harm.'

Ibid

There is no fascination so irresistible to a boy as the smile of a married woman.

Vivian Grey bk i, ch 7

At school friendship is a passion. It entrances the being; it tears the soul. All loves of after-life can never bring its rapture or its wretchedness ... It is a spell that can soften the acerbity of political warfare, and with its witchery can call forth a sigh even amid the callous bustle of fashionable saloons.

Coningsby bk i, ch 9

The irreclaimable and hopeless votary of lollypop, the opium eater of school boys.

Ibid

Buckhurst ... gave his opinion on the most refined dishes with all the intrepidity of saucy ignorance.

Coningsby bk i, ch 11

Youth is a blunder; Manhood a struggle; Old Age a regret.
Coningsby bk iii, ch 1

Almost everything that is great has been done by youth.
Ibid

The two greatest stimulants to action, Youth and Debt.
[Fakredeen] Tancred bk iii, ch 5

To do nothing and get something formed a boy's idea of a manly career.
Sybil bk i, ch 5

The Youth of a nation are the trustees of Posterity.
Sybil bk viii, ch 13

The microcosm of a public school.
Vivian Grey bk i, ch 2

The magic of our first love is our ignorance that it will ever end.
Henrietta Temple bk ii, ch 1

The blunders of youth are preferable to the triumphs of manhood and the successes of old age.
Lothair ch 31

I think myself that age is to a certain degree a habit.
R 95

When a man fell into his anecdotage it was a sign for him to retire from the world.
Lothair ch 28

Youth is, we all know, somewhat reckless in assertion and when we are young and curly one takes pride in sarcasm and invective.

H of C, 7 June 1839

The history of Heroes is the history of Youth.

Coningsby bk iii ch 1

When we are young, we think that not only ourselves but that all about us are immortal.

Venetia bk i ch 18

Youth, glittering youth! I remember when the prospect of losing my youth frightened me out of my wits. I dreamed of nothing but grey hairs, a paunch, and the gout or the gravel.

[Lord Cadurcis] Venetia bk vi ch 4

Youth, extreme youth, overthrew the Persian Empire.

Coningsby bk iii ch 1

The disappointed are always young.

DD 64